HOW DID WE FIND OUT . . . SERIES

Each of the books in this series on the history of science emphasizes the process of discovery.

"*How Did We Find Out*" Books by
Isaac Asimov

HOW DID WE FIND OUT THE
EARTH IS ROUND?

HOW DID WE FIND OUT ABOUT
ELECTRICITY?

HOW DID WE FIND OUT ABOUT
NUMBERS?

HOW DID WE FIND OUT

ABOUT NUMBERS?

Isaac Asimov
Illustrated by Daniel Nevins

WALKER AND COMPANY
New York

First published in the United States of America in 1973 by the Walker Publishing Company, Inc.

Published simultaneously in Canada by Fitzhenry & Whiteside, Limited, Toronto.

TRADE OSM: 0-8027-6135-6
REINF. ISBN: 0-8027-6136-4

LIBRARY OF CONGRESS CATALOG CARD NUMBER: 72-87350
PRINTED IN THE UNITED STATES OF AMERICA.

To Patti and Johnny Jeppson

CONTENTS

1 Numbers and FINGERS

MANY THOUSANDS OF YEARS AGO, when men asked the question, "How many?" they needed to have numbers.

Suppose you wanted to know how many sheep you had to make sure none had been lost. Suppose you wanted to know how many days had passed since something had happened. Suppose you wanted to know how many strangers were approaching a camp.

A person could show all he had of something or mention each object. If someone asked him how many days had passed since the last time the tribe had killed a bear, he could say, "A day and another day and another day and another day and another day."

That's rather clumsy. It would be easy to lose track.

Or else he could make a comparison with something else. He might notice that just near the river there was a group of trees. There was a tree and another tree and another tree and another tree and another tree. He could say, "The many days that have passed since the last time the tribe killed a bear is the same as the many trees that are in that clump over there."

That would really answer the question. By looking at the trees, someone could get an idea about how many days had passed.

But is a person always lucky enough to find a group of trees, flowers, rocks, or stars that are just as large as the group he is being asked about? Will he always be able to point to some handy group and say, "That many".?

It would be very nice if he could arrange to have groups of different sizes always near him. Then whenever there was a how-many question, he could pick out the right group and say, "That many."

Almost any person who thought about how convenient it would be to have such groups would be likely to think of the fingers on his hands. Nothing could be more convenient than a person's own hands which are always with him.

Look at your hands. Each one has a finger and another finger and another finger and another finger and another finger. You could hold up your hand and point to the fingers and say, "The many days that have passed since the last time the tribe killed a bear is the same as the many fingers I have on my hand."

You can give a name to each finger. We call the one that sticks out by itself the *thumb*. The one next to the thumb is the *forefinger*, the next one is the *middle finger*, the next is the *ring finger* and finally there is the *little finger*.

You can hold up as many fingers as you want. You

could hold up the forefinger and bend all the other fingers out of the way and say, "This many." Or you could hold up a forefinger and a middle finger and say, "This many." You could hold up all the fingers on one hand and the forefinger on the other and say, "This many," and so on.

It would be nice, however, if you didn't have to hold up your hands to show combinations of fingers. You might be carrying something you didn't want to put down. It might be cold and you might not want to expose your fingers to the icy wind. It might be dark so that no one could see your fingers anyway.

Suppose you made up a word for each combination of fingers. For example, instead of holding up the forefinger only and saying, "This many," you could use the word, "One." Then instead of having to hold up the forefinger and saying, "I have this

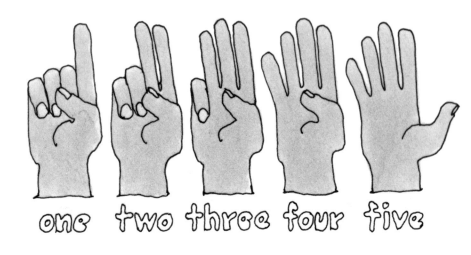

one   two   three   four   five

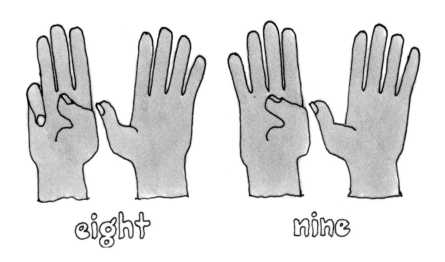

eight   nine

14

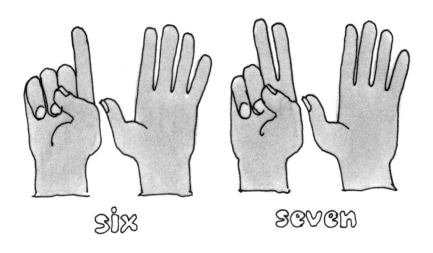

six   seven

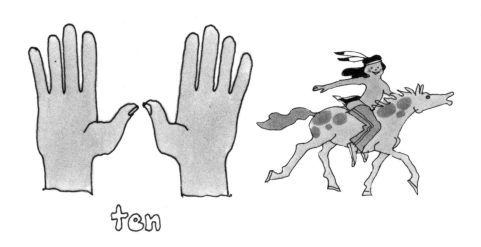

ten

many knives," you could say, "I have one knife." You could say that with your hands in your pocket or in the dark and people would still understand.

Why should you use the word one? Why not some other word? Nobody really knows. The word was made up so many thousands of years ago that we don't know how it came about. It was used long before the modern languages of Europe developed. Each modern European language uses a different version of the word but they are all similar.

In English we say *one*, in French the word is *un*, in Spanish it is *uno*, in German it is *ein*, in Latin it is *unus*, in Greek it is *monos*. All the words have the letter *n* in it. They all come from some original word we no longer know.

We won't worry about the original word, however, or about the words used in other languages. We'll just use the English words with which we are familiar.

For the combination of forefinger and middle finger, we say two. Forefinger, middle finger, and ring finger is three. Then we say four, five, six, seven, eight, nine, and ten.

The word ten is used when we hold up both hands with all the fingers stretched out and say, "This is how many I have."

Once people get used to these words, it becomes very simple to describe "how many." You can say, "I saw you six days ago," or "Bring in eight logs for the fire," or "Give me two arrows."

Then, suppose someone drops a bunch of arrows at your feet and says, "Here are some arrows. I don't know how many there are." You can then count them. You can pick up an arrow and say, "One." You can pick up another and say, "Two." If when you pick up the last arrow you say, "Seven," that means there are seven arrows. Because you have ten fingers altogether, you have ten different words used for answering questions of "how many?" Such words are called *numbers*.

But it is quite easy to have a group made up of more than ten things. Suppose you had a bunch of arrows and picked them up one by one, counting as you did so. Finally you picked up an arrow and said, "Ten," but found there were still some arrows on the ground. What do you do now? You need more numbers. If you keep on making up new names for numbers, it is hard to remember them all. Ten different numbers—one, two, three, four, five, six, seven, eight, nine, and ten—are quite enough to remember.

But suppose you use those numbers to make up new numbers in some sensible way. Then it would be easy to remember the new numbers.

For instance, you might pick up ten arrows and find that there is still one left on the ground. You can say, "There are one-left arrows." As it happens, the number word eleven is a form of a very old English word meaning "one left."

In the same way, twelve is a form of a very old English word meaning "two left."

After that it is even easier. Thirteen is a slightly twisted way of writing "three and ten." If you wrote "threeteen" that would be quite close to writing thirteen.

Fourteen is even closer to "four and ten" and then

there is fifteen, sixteen, seventeen, eighteen, and nineteen.

Nineteen is "nine and ten." One more than that is "ten and ten." That's "two-tens," isn't it? And in fact the number after nineteen is twenty which is a form of an old word that meant "two-tens."

After that we have twenty-one, which is "two-tens and one." Then twenty-two, twenty-three, and so on until twenty-nine which is "two-tens and nine." The number after that is "two-tens and ten" which is the same as saying "three-tens" and that's what thirty means.

If we keep on making up words for larger and larger numbers we come to thirty-nine which is followed by forty ("four-tens"). Then we come to fifty, sixty, seventy, eighty, and ninety.

Finally we come to ninety-nine which is "nine-tens and nine." The number after that is "ten-tens." Every time you come to ten of something, a new word is invented. (Remember that the number ten is important because of the ten fingers on the two hands.) For that reason "ten-tens" is called one hundred. It comes from an old, old word we don't use any more.

We can go on making larger numbers. We can speak of one hundred and one, one hundred and eleven, one hundred and thirty-three, and one hundred and sixty-eight. When we reach one hundred and ninety-nine, the next number is two hundred.

We can go on to three hundred, four hundred, and so on. By the time we reach ten hundred we need another new word. (For ten hundred we say one thousand.) And we can go on to two thousand, three thousand and so on.

There are still larger number-words, but the still larger ones were made up in modern times. In ancient times it was hardly ever necessary to go beyond the word thousand, so we'll stop there.

2 Numbers and WRITING

NOBODY KNOWS when numbers were first invented but certainly it was before anyone had invented writing. The time came, however, when people needed to work out a system for making marks that stood for words. This happened about five thousand years ago in the land we now call Iraq. Two rivers flow through that land, the Euphrates and the Tigris. Near the place where they reach the sea there was an ancient land we call Sumeria. It was the Sumerians who first made use of writing. Other ancient people, the Chinese and the Egyptians, also developed systems of writing. Gradually writing spread all over the world.

When writing was invented, the Sumerians and the Egyptians had cities, temples, and farmland irrigation ditches. Many people had to cooperate in the building of these marks of civilization. They all had to contribute time and effort. They also had to pay taxes.

It therefore became important to keep records. The priests of the temples were in charge of such things. They had to make sure they knew who paid taxes and how much. They could memorize it, perhaps, but memory could play tricks and there might be arguments. It was better to make some markings that would show the state of the taxes in a permanent way. In case of argument the markings could be looked at.

SUMERIAN WRITING

When writing was first invented the priests used a different marking for each word. This meant there were a lot of markings to memorize so learning how to read and write was very hard. In very ancient times only the priests could read and write.

One of the most important sets of markings that had to be made was for the different numbers. After all, any records you keep will have to be full of numbers—so many of this, so many of that.

You could make a different marking for every different number but there are so many different numbers that this would mean remembering thousands of different markings.

But since the fingers were used in connection with the invention of number-words, why not let the number one be represented by a straight vertical mark that looks like a finger? That is what the Egyptians did, for instance. They made a mark like this, I, and that stood for one.

Any mark or symbol that is used to represent a number is called a *numeral.* The symbol I is an example of an Egyptian numeral. Other people used the same symbol or one very like it since everybody who thought of one drew a picture of one finger.

It isn't important what the exact symbols are, however. What is important is how they are used. We can understand this better if we use symbols that are familiar to us. For the number one we can use the symbol I.

Suppose now we want to write a symbol for two. Instead of inventing a brand-new numeral, why not write II? This looks just like two fingers.

Writing the next few numbers is easy: III is three, IIII is four, IIIII is five and so on all the way up to IIIIIIIII for nine.

The advantage of this is that we know exactly what number the symbols stand for by counting the I's. The disadvantage is that when there are a considerable number of I's it is wearisome to write them and to count them. It is also easy to make a mistake in writing them or in counting them.

The Egyptians usually wrote the symbols in some sort of pattern. For five they didn't write IIIII, they wrote III and then wrote II immediately underneath. It was easier to see three marks and two marks than to make out five marks in a row. In the same way they wrote nine not as IIIIIIIII but as three III's, one group under the other.

Even dividing numerals into groups, however, will not help as we go into larger and larger numbers. Imagine writing fifty-four as
IIIIIIIIIIIIIIIIIIIIIIIIIIIIIIIIIIIIIIIIIIIIIIIIIIIIII.

What the Egyptians did was to invent a new symbol for ten. For this they used a symbol like an upside-down U. We don't have to use that symbol, however, to show how the Egyptian numerals worked. Suppose instead we use the symbol T for ten. That would make it particularly clear to us because in our language T is the first letter of the word ten.

If you wanted to write eleven you could write it TI or IT. It doesn't matter which one you write. It is either ten and one or one and ten. In either case the number is eleven. You could have TII for twelve or IIT or even ITI. In any combination the symbols add up to twelve.

It would be more convenient, however, to use some regular system. Then people would get used to it and be able to understand the numbers that much more easily. We could put all the large numerals on the left and all the small ones on the right.

In that case twenty-three would be TTIII (ten and ten and one and one and one). Seventy-four would be TTTTTTTIIII and ninety-nine would be TTTTTTTTTIIIIIIIII. Of course the T's and I's would be arranged in patterns to make it easier to count them.

The Egyptians decided that no more than nine of any symbol should be written or counted and so they invented a new symbol every time ten of any symbol had to be written.

To write one hundred you might write ten of the symbols for ten like this: TTTTTTTTTT. Instead of doing that, a new symbol was invented to stand for one hundred. The Egyptians used a kind of curl which looks a little like this: 9.

We don't need to use that, however. Instead let's call the symbol for one hundred H since that is the first letter of the word in our own language.

Three hundred and thirty-three can be written HHHTTTIII. Seven hundred and eighteen can be written HHHHHHHTIIIIIIII and eight hundred and ninety can be written HHHHHHHHTTTTTTTTT. You can write any number with these three symbols up to nine hundred and ninety-nine, which is HHHHHHHHHTTTTTTTTTIIIIIIIII.

For all the numbers from one to nine hundred and ninety-nine you need to memorize only three different symbols and you have to count each symbol no higher than nine. To write one thousand you would have to write ten symbols for one hundred so a new symbol is invented. Another new symbol is invented for ten thousand and still another for one hundred thousand and so on.

You can go as high as you want in numbers by this method, inventing a new symbol every time you need ten of a lower symbol.

3 Numbers and the ROMANS

THE EGYPTIAN SYSTEM of numerals gave special importance to the number ten because that was the total number of fingers on two hands.

The Mayans, a people who lived in southern Mexico in the days before the Europeans came, used a system based on twenty. There are twenty fingers and toes on your hands and feet. (In our own language we have some of that since we use *score* to represent twenty. We can say that there are "two-score and fourteen" people present, meaning "fifty-four." In the Gettysburg Address, President Lincoln began, "Four-score and seven years ago," meaning "eighty-seven years ago.")

However, it is also possible to give twelve special importance. The number twelve is more convenient in some ways than ten. Ten can be divided only by two and five. If you group things by tens it isn't possible to divide them evenly into thirds and quarters. Twelve, however, can be divided by two, three, four, and six.

Some of the importance of twelve is shown by our

MAYAN COUNTING
HIS TOES

use of the word *dozen*. For example, we speak of a dozen eggs. Half a dozen is six; a third of a dozen is four; a fourth of a dozen is three; a sixth of a dozen is two. We go on to sell things in dozens of dozens. A dozen dozen is twelve twelves, which comes to one hundred and forty-four. We call that a *gross* from a French word meaning large.

The Sumerians gave special importance to sixty. That can be divided by still more numbers than twelve can. We also give importance to sixty in our own lives. We have sixty seconds in a minute, for example, and sixty minutes in an hour.

The larger the number we base our system on, the more particular symbols we might have to count when we write the numbers. Suppose the Egyptians invented a new symbol only when they had to use twelve of some smaller symbol instead of ten. Then we might have to count eleven symbols instead of only nine. Using twenty or sixty would be even worse.

Suppose we used a number smaller than ten, though. We might use five, for example, since this is the total number of fingers on one hand.

About two thousand years ago, large sections of Europe, Asia, and Africa were ruled from the city of Rome. This "Roman Empire" used a system of numerals based on five.

The Romans used symbols taken from their alphabet. Fortunately, the people of Europe and America use the Roman alphabet so the Roman symbols are familiar to us.

The Romans began by letting one be written as I. For two, three, and four they had II, III, and IIII. So far it looks like the Egyptian system but the Romans only allowed four of any symbol to be used before inventing a new symbol. Instead of writing five as the Egyptian IIIII they wrote it as V.

Instead of writing six as IIIIII they wrote it VI. Nine was VIIII. If they wrote ten as VIIIII, that would mean five of the symbol I and they didn't allow that. They used a new symbol for ten which was X.

32

BLACK SEA

RANEAN SEA

Empire ✶

33

The list of symbols up to one thousand is as follows:

I = one
V = five
X = ten
L = fifty
C = one hundred
D = five hundred
M = one thousand

By using special symbols for five, fifty and five hundred, the Romans never had to use more than four of any of the symbols for one, ten, or one hundred.

To write twenty-two they wrote XXII. Seventy-three is LXXIII. Four hundred and eighteen is CCCCXVIII. One thousand nine hundred and ninety-nine is MDCCCCLXXXXVIIII.

If you try to write one thousand nine hundred and ninety-nine by the Egyptian system, you would need one "thousand" symbol, and nine symbols each for "hundred," "ten," and "one." That would mean twenty-eight symbols all together. In Roman numerals only sixteen symbols are needed.

The Egyptian system uses only four different kinds of symbols while the Roman system uses seven. In the Roman system you need less counting but more memorizing.

When these Roman numerals were first developed it didn't matter in what order the symbols were placed. Whether you wrote XVI or XIV, or IXV, or VIX, it all came to sixteen. No matter what the order in which you add ten, five and one you end up with sixteen.

Of course, it is easier to add up a number if you arrange the symbols according to some convenient system. The usual way is to put all the symbols of the same sort together. The largest symbol is on the left and as you move to the right you write down smaller and smaller symbols. Thus seventy-eight would always be written LXXVIII, working down from L to X to V to I.

The later Romans thought of a way of still further decreasing the number of a particular symbol that had to be written down. As long as symbols were always written from left to right and from large to small why not sometimes reverse the order?

When you put the smaller symbol after the larger one in the usual way you add the two. Therefore, VI is "five plus one" or six. If on the other hand you put the smaller symbol *before* the larger one you *subtract* it from the larger. In this way IV is "five minus one" or four.

By writing four as IV instead of IIII you have to write and read only two symbols instead of four, but you have to notice the positions and remember to subtract instead of add.

In the same way, XL is forty while LX is sixty and XC is ninety while CX is one hundred and ten and CM is nine hundred while MC is one thousand one hundred.

The year nineteen seventy-three can be written MCMLXXIII instead of MDCCCCLXXIII—eight symbols instead of twelve. One thousand nine hundred ninety-nine can be written MCMXCIX instead of MDCCCCLXXXXVIIII—seven symbols instead of sixteen.

Of course, once you start using the subtracting notion, you can't scramble the order of the symbols anymore. It becomes important to place each symbol exactly.

The western part of the Roman Empire broke up just about one thousand five hundred years ago. The people of western Europe kept on using Roman numerals for more than seven hundred years after the Roman Empire had come to an end.

4 Numbers and ALPHABETS

WE HAVE TO REPEAT SYMBOLS in both the Egyptian and Roman system of numerals. We always have to have combinations like III or XX or TTTTT. That means we have to count the symbols and that we might make a mistake.

Is there any way of never using any symbol more than once in any number? If we want to do that we have to use a large number of symbols. If we don't want two to be II we have to give it a special symbol. The same with three and with four and so on.

It would seem that this isn't so good since we would have to do a lot of memorizing. But suppose the symbols were *already* memorized.

About three thousand four hundred years ago, a people called the Phoenicians, who lived in what is now the country of Lebanon on the east shore of the Mediterranean Sea, invented the alphabet. They devised a series of letters, each with a different sound. Out of these letters any word could be formed.

The alphabet spread in all directions. It spread to the Hebrews and to the Greeks, for instance. Everyone who learned how to write (and this became

much simpler with an alphabet) had to memorize the alphabet. Of course, the names of the letters were different in different languages, but each group of people memorized the letters in its own language.

Hebrew children, in learning the alphabet, learned to say: *aleph, beth, gimmel, daled, hay, vuv,* and so on. Greek children learned to say, *alpha, beta, gamma, delta, epsilon, zeta, eta,* and so on. Children who speak Englisn learn to say, *ay, bee, see, dee, ee, ef, gee,* and so on.

The alphabet is learned so well that it becomes automatic for anyone who can write. All the letters are known in the exact order and each one has a symbol.

Why not let the symbols for the letters serve as symbols for the numbers also? You can let the first letter stand for the first number, the second letter for the second number, the third letter for the third number, and so on. You don't have to learn a single new symbol. You know all the symbols already.

The Hebrew letters and the Greek letters are quite different from our own but we don't have to bother with those letters. We're just interested in this system of writing numerals which both the Greeks and Hebrews used. We can just as well use our own alphabet to see how it works.

Using our own alphabet we can say that:

A = one
B = two
C = three
D = four
E = five
F = six
G = seven
H = eight
I = nine
J = ten

If we keep on going this way, we'll only reach the number twenty-six since there are only twenty-six letters in the alphabet.

However, we can start combining. We can write eleven as "ten-one" or JA. Twelve would be "ten-two" or JB. In the same way we could go on with JC for thirteen, JD for fourteen, JE for fifteen, JF for sixteen, JG for seventeen, JH for eighteen and JI for nineteen.

We could write JJ for twenty, but now we would be repeating symbols. Instead we go on to the next letter and let K stand for twenty. In fact, starting with J, we could go on like this:

J = ten
K = twenty
L = thirty
M = forty
N = fifty
O = sixty
P = seventy
Q = eighty
R = ninety

S = one hundred
T = two hundred
U = three hundred
V = four hundred
W = five hundred
X = six hundred
Y = seven hundred
Z = eight hundred

We've run out of the alphabet now but we can make up a symbol just to carry things to nine hundred. We can let that be written as £, for instance.

By this system of numerals we can write any number under a thousand with one, two, or three symbols and in no number will any symbol be repeated.

Seventy-five is PE, one hundred and fifty-six is SNF, eight hundred and two is ZB, nine hundred and ninety-nine is £RI. You can write all the numbers from one to nine and ninety-nine yourself by this system. You will find it is very easy.

If you want to go beyond nine hundred and ninety-nine you can make special marks. A little bar over a letter might multiply everything by a thousand. In this way, $\overline{A}$ would be one thousand, $\overline{B}$ would be two thousand and so on. Five thousand eight hundred and twenty-one would be $\overline{E}$ZKA.

One bad point about using the same symbols for letters and numerals is that it makes numbers look like words.

For instance, using our own alphabet, the symbol for five hundred and sixty-five is WOE. That hap-

pens to be a word that means sorrow. For that reason, people might decide that five hundred and sixty-five is a bad-luck number.

They might create a whole system for deciding what numbers mean according to the letters used as symbols. The Greek and Hebrew people both did

this and invented a kind of numerology that was just silly nonsense.

We still have this numerology today and many people are foolish enough to believe in it. It all got started because the Greeks and Hebrews used the same symbols for letters and numbers.

5 Numbers and "NOTHING"

IT MIGHT BE BETTER if we used a different symbol for each of the numbers but *didn't* use letters of the alphabet. Suppose we invented completely different symbols.

The Hindu people of India developed a set of symbols for numbers and today we use them. The forms we use aren't quite the same as the ones the Hindus had many centuries ago. Still if we look at the old Hindu numerals we can see the beginnings of the numerals we now use. From the Hindus we get the following:

1 = one
2 = two
3 = three
4 = four
5 = five
6 = six
7 = seven
8 = eight
9 = nine

These numerals, or their original ancestors, first

appeared in India about two thousand two hundred years ago.

You might wonder how we came to use numbers like the Hindus. Aren't they, after all, just another set of symbols? Wouldn't people rather stick to the old symbols such as the Roman numerals they were used to?

Yes, people would! They did stick to the old symbols just as long as they could. However, the reason why the Hindu numerals started spreading beyond India was that the Hindu people had come up with a better idea.

To begin with the Hindus (like the Egyptians) made up new symbols for the numbers higher than nine. They had different symbols for ten, twenty, thirty, and so on; also for one hundred, two hundred, three hundred, and so on.

But then someone (and of course we don't know who) must have asked himself why this was necessary. The number two hundred means two "one hundreds." The number twenty means two "tens." The number two means two "ones." In each case the number means two of something.

Suppose you make up your mind the symbol on the extreme right of a numeral tells you how many ones there are. The symbol to its left tells you how many tens there are. The symbol next to the left tells you how many one hundreds there are, and so on. The meaning of a symbol depends on the position it is in. In this way the nine Hindu numerals—1, 2, 3, 4, 5, 6, 7, 8, 9—might be enough.

Suppose you have the numeral 354. The right-

most symbol tells you that there are four ones or four. The one to its left tells you that there are five tens or fifty. The one to its left tells you there are three one hundreds or three hundred. Four and fifty and three hundred add up to three hundred fifty-four and that is what 354 stands for.

Any number can be read that way. The number 18 stands for one ten and eight ones, which comes to ten and eight, or eighteen. The number 999 stands for nine one hundreds, nine tens and nine ones. This is nine hundred and ninety and nine, or nine hundred and ninety-nine.

You can go as high as you want in the Hindu system. A number like 87235 means, if you work from right to left, five ones, three tens, two one hundreds, seven one thousands and eight ten thousands. Add these up and you come out with eighty-seven thousand two hundred and thirty-five. You are still using the nine Hindu numerals and nothing else. But there's a catch.

Suppose you wanted to write the number two thousand and three. This is made up of two "one thousands" and three "ones." There are no one hundreds at all and no tens either.

Can you write it 23, standing for two "one thousands" and three "ones?" If you do this, how do you know the 2 stands for two "one thousands?" Maybe it stands for two "one hundreds" or for two "tens."

Maybe you could leave a space to show that the "one hundreds" and the "tens" are absent. You could write 2 3. Then someone would see that the "one hundreds" and the "tens" are skipped so that the 2 must stand for two "one thousands."

But how can a person be sure that the empty space holds two empty columns? Maybe it only holds one. Maybe it holds three.

No, leaving an empty space isn't enough. You must have some symbol that stands for "no tens at all" or "no hundreds at all."

It was a very difficult thing, however, to get the notion that such a symbol was needed. It took thousands of years after human beings started using number symbols for anyone to think of writing a symbol that stands for "nothing."

We don't know exactly who it was who finally thought of using such a symbol. We think it was a Hindu. We don't know for sure when it happened. Maybe it was about a thousand three hundred years ago.

The symbol we now use for "nothing" is just a circle with nothing in it. It is 0. The Hindus called it *sunya* meaning "nothing."

Let's see how this "nothing" works. If we want to write twenty-three we see that this means two "tens" and three "ones" and we write it 23.

If we want to write two hundred and three, we have two "one hundreds," no tens at all, and three "ones." We therefore write it 203.

How about two thousand and thirty? That is two "one thousands," no one hundreds at all, three "tens" and no ones at all. It is written 2030.

You can work out for yourself why two thousand three hundred is 2300 and why two thousand and three is 2003.

For that matter ten is one "ten" and no ones at all so it is written 10.

Using the nine Hindu symbols 1, 2, 3, 4, 5, 6, 7, 8, 9, and the symbol for "nothing," 0, any number at all can be written easily. There is never any doubt what column each symbol is in.

6 Numbers and the WORLD

THERE IS NO DOUBT that the Hindu system of numerals, including the symbol for "nothing" is the best ever invented. You can write big numbers with only a few symbols and you don't have to memorize more than ten symbols altogether no matter how large a number you have to write. Nor do you make words out of numbers and get confused.

Most important of all, it turned out to be easier to do arithmetic with numerals written according to the Hindu system than according to any other system ever invented.

In ancient times, only people who had studied mathematics a long time could divide numbers using either Roman numerals or Greek numerals. Using the Hindu system, school children can learn to divide without much trouble. If you think long division is hard, just try doing it with Roman numerals!

Once people discovered how much easier it was to do arithmetic with the Hindu numerals they used them also. The Hindu system began to spread.

About 800 A.D., not very long after the symbol for

"nothing" was invented, the Hindu numerals spread into the lands north and west of India. These lands were inhabited by people who spoke Arabic. Arabic-speaking people also lived all across northern Africa and in Spain as well. The Hindu numerals spread through Africa and into Spain.

The Arabs called the Hindu *sunya*, the symbol for "nothing," *sifr*.

About 820, an Arabic mathematician named Muhammed Al-Khwarizmi (al-KWAR-iz-mee) wrote an important book on mathematics. He was the first to give full instructions on how to use the Hindu numerals in arithmetic.

Over a hundred years later, a Frenchman named Gerbert (zhare-BARE) was very interested in gathering knowledge. At that time, France, England, and Germany were in a "Dark Age." There were few schools and books and hardly anyone could even read and write. Spain, however, which was under the control of the Arabs was much more advanced.

Gerbert traveled to Spain in 967 and studied books in Arabic. He came across Al-Khwarizmi's book and was struck with the convenience of the new system of numerals. He brought them back to France with him. The people in Europe called them *Arabic numerals* because they obtained them from Arabic-speaking people. The people in Europe did not know they came from India to begin with. We still call the numbers 1, 2, 3, and so on Arabic numerals today.

Since Gerbert became Pope under the name of Sylvester II in 999, you would think Europeans would listen to him. They didn't. A few other

learned men recommended the new Arabic numerals. However, the Europeans of the time were using Roman numerals and were used to them. Even though the Roman numerals were very clumsy and made arithmetic very difficult, the Europeans stuck with them.

Two more centuries passed. Then we come to
Leonardo Fibonacci (fee-boh-NAHT-chee), a man
who lived in an Italian city called Pisa. He picked up
the notion of the Hindu system of numerals while he
was visiting northern Africa. In 1202, he published a
book in which he used Arabic numerals plus the symbol for "nothing." He showed how it could be used
in arithmetic.

By that time, Europe had emerged from the Dark
Age. People were more prosperous and more
learned. In Italy, especially, there were many businessmen who had to do a lot of calculating to keep
track of their dealings. As Italian businessmen found

how convenient the Arabic numerals were they abandoned the Roman numerals and used the new system instead. They could see that the symbol for "nothing" was most important. They used the Arabic word *sifr*. Then they changed it to *zepiro* since it was easier to pronounce and looked more natural.

The word zepiro becomes *zero* to us and that is our most common word for the symbol 0. An English word sometimes applied to it, and almost as familiar is *naught* meaning "nothing."

From Italy, Arabic numerals began to spread through the rest of Europe. By the time Columbus discovered America all of Europe was using Arabic numerals.

We still use Roman numerals, however, when we want to be impressive and when we don't need them to do arithmetic. Queen Elizabeth of England is the second English queen to have that name. She is therefore called Elizabeth II. Pope Paul is the sixth pope of that name so he is Paul VI.

It is not only Europe, though, that uses Arabic numerals now. In the last century, those numerals have spread everywhere. In dozens of strange languages using strange symbols for their letters and words you will find the familiar, 1, 2, 3, 4, 5, 6, 7, 8, 9, and 0.

And the whole thing started when some primitive man wondered how to describe how many stone axes he had and looked at his fingers to see if they would help.

INDEX